USEFUL EXPRESSIONS

in DUTCH

FOR THE ENGLISH-SPEAKING TOURIST

Editors: A. Z. Stern — Joseph A. Reif, Ph.D.

·K·U·P·E·R·A·R·D·

© 1991 KS-JM Books

Distributed in the United Kingdom by:
Kuperard (London) Ltd.
30 Cliff Road
London NW1 9AG

ISBN 1-870668-76-6

This booklet is an up-to-date and practical phrase book for your trip to the Netherlands. It includes the phrases and vocabulary you will need in most of the situations in which you will find yourself, and it contains a pronunciation guide for all the material. Some of the phrases occur in more than one section so that you do not have to turn pages back and forth. At the beginning is a basic, general vocabulary with which you should become familiar, and at the end is a list of emergency expressions for quick reference.

The pronunciation of Dutch is fairly simple. With only a few exceptions the sounds are very similar to English sounds, and you will quickly achieve an easily understandable accent. The transcription, when read as if it were English, will give a close approximation to normal Dutch. Special attention should be paid to the following vowels and consonants:

a as in f**a**ther

ew when short, is pronounced like the **i** of b**i**t, but with rounded lips; when long, it is pronounced like the **ee** of b**ee**t, but with rounded lips.

aew is a diphthong composed of the **a** of **a**bout followed by the **ew** described above.

oo as in b**oo**t or f**oo**d

ow as in c**ow**, not as in l**ow**

kh like the **ch** in Scottish lo**ch**

r is trilled

zh like the **g** in bei**g**e

Words borrowed from English and pronounced more or less as in English are given in the English spelling and marked in single quotes, e.g., 'grapefruit'.

In words ending in **en**, particularly verbs and plurals, the **n** is frequently dropped in normal speech.

Stressed syllables are printed in **boldface**.

CONTENTS

BASIC DICTIONARY	GEWONE WOORDEN	KHEVOHNE VORDE
Thank you	Dank u	dahnk ew
Thank you very much	Dank u vriendelijk	dahnk ew **vreen**delik
Please	Alstublieft	alstu**bleeft**
Excuse me	Pardon	par**doh**
Never mind	Geeft niets	khayft neets
What? What is that?	Wat? Wat is dat?	vat? vat is dat?
Where? Where is that?	Waar? Waar is dat?	vahr? vahr is dat?
When? How?	Wanneer? Hoe?	va**nayr**? hoo?
Which? Why?	Welke? Waarom?	**vel**ke? vah**rom**?
Is that?	Is dat?	is dat?
That is not	Dat is niet	dat is neet
Yes, no, perhaps	Ja, nee, misschien	yah, nay, mis-**kheen**
Correct, incorrect	Juist, niet juist	yaewst, neet yaewst
So so	Zo zo	zoh zoh
Good, bad	Goed, slecht	khoot, slekht
No good, not bad	Niet goed, niet slecht	neet khoot, neet slekht
There is, there is not (none)	Er is, er is niet	er is, er is neet

1

I, you	Ik, u	ik, ew
He, she	Hij, zij	hay, zay
We, you	Wij, u	vay, ew
They	Zij	zay
Mine, yours	Mijn, uw	mayn, ew
Ours, theirs	Onze, hun	**onze**, hewn
At my place, at your place	Bij mij, bij u	bay may, bay ew
Wet, dry	Nat, droog	naht, drohkh
Old, new	Oud, nieuw	owt, new
Pretty, ugly	Mooi, niet mooi	**moh**-ee, neet **moh**-ee
Much, few	Veel, weinig	vayl, **vay**nikh
How many? How much?	Hoe veel?	hoo vayl?
Cheap, expensive	Goedkoop, duur	khoot-**kohp**, dewr
Very expensive	Erg duur	erkh dewr
Free (of charge)	Gratis	**khrah**tis
More, less	Meer, minder	mayr, **min**der
Cheaper, more expensive	Goedkoper, duurder	khoot-**koper**, **dewr**der
Heavy, light	Zwaar, licht	zvahr, likht

Now, at the same time as...	Nu, even laat als	new, ayven **laht** als
During	Gedurende	khe**dew**rende
Early, late	Vroeg, laat	vrookh, laht
On time, in time	Op tijd	op tayt
Here, there	Hier, daar	heer, dahr
Inside, outside	Binnen, buiten	**binnen**, **baew**ten
Up (stairs), down (stairs)	Boven, beneden	**boh**ven, be**nay**den
To...	Naar	nahr
Near, far	Dicht bij, ver weg	dikht bay, ver vekh
In front of	Voor	vohr
Behind (after)	Achter	**akh**ter
Sky	Hemel	**hay**mel
Sun, moon	Zon, maan	zon, mahn
Stars	Sterren	**steh**ren
Light, darkness	Licht, duister	likht, **daew**ster
Heat, cold, warm	Hitte, koud, warm	**hitte**, kowt, vahrm
East, west	Oost, west	ohst, vest
North, south	Noord, zuid	nohrt, zaewt

Rain, snow, wind	Regen, sneeuw, wind	**ray**khen, **snay**ew, vint
Earth, mountain, valley	Aarde, berg, dal	**ahr**de, berkh, dahl
River, bridge	Rivier, brug	re**veer**, brookh
Desert, sand	Woestijn, zand	voo**stayn**, zahnt
Sea, water, ship	Zee, water, schip	zay, **vah**ter, skhip
Country, place	Land, plaats	lahnt, plahts
City, village	Stad, dorp	stat, dorp
Road, street	Weg, straat	vekh, straht
House, flat	Huis, flat	haewss, 'flat'
Room, door	Kamer, deur	**kah**mer, dayr
Key, lock	Sleutel, slot	**slay**tel, slot
Wall, window	Muur, raam	mewr, rahm
Roof, steps	Dak, trap	dak, trap
Kitchen, toilet	Keuken, W.C.	**kerr**ken, vay-say
Bed, pillows	Bed, kussens	bet, **kews**sens
Blanket, carpet	Deken, kleed	**day**ken, klayt
Table, chair	Tafel, stoel	**tah**fel, stool
Man, woman	Man, vrouw	man, vrow

4

English	Dutch	Pronunciation
Father, mother	Vader, moeder	**vah**der, **moo**der
Son, daughter	Zoon, dochter	zohn, **dokh**ter
Grandson, granddaughter	Kleinzoon, kleindochter	**klayn**zohn, **klayn**dokhter
Brother, sister	Broer, zuster	broor, **zew**ster
Uncle, aunt	Oom, tante	ohm, **tahn**te
Husband, wife	Man, vrouw	man, vrow
Boy, girl	Jongen, meisje	**yong**en, **may**she
Old man, old woman	Oude man, oude vrouw	**ow**de man, **ow**de vrow
To want	Willen	**vil**len
I want, You want	Ik wil, u wilt	ik vil, ew vilt
I wanted, you wanted	Ik wilde, u wilde	ik **vil**de, ew **vil**de
I will want, you will want	Ik zal willen, u zult willen	ik zahl **vil**len, ew zewlt **vil**len
I do not want	Ik wil niet	ik vil neet
To visit	Bezoeken	be**zoo**ken
I visit, you visit	Ik bezoek, u bezoekt	ik be**zook**, ew be**zookt**
I visited, you visited	Ik bezocht, u bezocht	ik be**zokht**, ew be**zokht**
I will visit, you will visit	Ik zal bezoeken, u zult bezoeken	ik zahl be**zoo**ken, ew zewlt be**zoo**ken

To speak	Spreken	**spray**ken
I speak, you speak	Ik spreek, u spreekt	ik sprayk, ew spraykt
I spoke, you spoke	Ik sprak, u sprak	ik sprahk, ew sprahk
I will speak, you will speak	Ik zal spreken, u zult spreken	ik zahl **spray**ken, ew zewlt **spray**ken
I do not speak	Ik spreek niet	ik sprayk neet
To understand	Verstaan	ver**stahn**
I understand, you understand	Ik versta, u verstaat	ik ver**stah**, ew ver**staht**
I understood, you understood	ik verstond, u verstond	ik ver**stond**, ew ver**stond**
I do not understand	Ik begrijp niet	ik be**khrayp** neet
To go	Gaan	khahn
I go, you go	Ik ga, u gaat	ik khah, ew khaht
I went, you went	Ik ging, u ging	ik khing, ew khing
I will go, you will go	Ik zal gaan, u zult gaan	ik zahl khahn, ew zewlt khahn
I do not go	Ik ga niet	ik khah neet
To travel	Reizen	**ray**zen
I travel, you travel	Ik reis, u reist	ik rayss, ew raysst
I travelled, you travelled	Ik reisde, u reisde	ik **rayz**de, ew **rayz**de

English	Dutch	Pronunciation
I will travel, you will travel	Ik zal reizen, u zult reizen	ik zahl **ray**zen, ew zewlt **ray**zen
I do not travel	Ik reis niet	ik rayss neet
To stand	Staan	stahn
I stand, you stand	Ik sta, u staat	ik stah, ew staht
I stood, you stood	Ik stond, u stond	ik stond, ew stond
I will stand, you will stand	Ik zal staan, u zult staan	ik zahl stahn, ew zewlt stahn
I do not stand	Ik sta niet	ik stah neet
To sleep	Slapen	**slahp**en
I sleep, you sleep	Ik slaap, u slaapt	ik slahp, ew slahpt
I slept, you slept	Ik sliep, u sliep	ik sleep, ew sleep
I will sleep, you will sleep	Ik zal slapen, u zult slapen	ik zahl **slah**pen, ew zewlt **slah**pen
I do not sleep	Ik slaap niet	ik slahp neet
To rest	Rusten	**rews**ten
I rest, you rest	Ik rust, u rust	ik rewst, ew rewst
I rested, you rested	Ik rustte, u rustte	ik rewste, ew rewste
I will rest, you will rest	Ik zal rusten, u zult rusten	ik zahl **rews**ten, ew zewlt **rews**ten

I do not rest	Ik rust niet	ik rewst neet
To eat	Eten	**ay**ten
I eat, you eat	Ik eet, u eet	ik ayt, ew ayt
I ate, you ate	Ik at, u at	ik aht, ew aht
I will eat, you will eat	Ik zal eten, u zult eten	ik zahl **ay**ten, ew zewlt **ay**ten
I do not eat	Ik eet niet	ik ayt neet
To drink	Drinken	**drink**en
I drink, you drink	Ik drink, u drinkt	ik drink, ew drinkt
I drank, you drank	Ik dronk, u dronk	ik dronk, ew dronk
I will drink, you will drink	Ik zal drinken, u zult drinken	ik zahl **drink**en, ew zewlt **drink**en
I do not drink	Ik drink niet	ik drink neet
To be afraid	Bang zijn	bahng zayn
I am afraid, you are afraid	Ik ben bang, u bent bang	ik ben bahng, ew bent bahng
I was afraid, you were afraid	Ik was bang, u was bang	ik vas bahng, ew vas bahng
I will be afraid	Ik zal bang zijn	ik zahl bahng zayn
You will be afraid	U zult bang zijn	ew zewlt bahng zayn
I am not afraid	Ik ben niet bang	ik ben neet bahng

To hurry	Haasten	**hahs**ten
I am in a hurry	Ik haast mij	ik hahst may
You are in a hurry	U haast u	ew hahst ew
I hurried, you hurried	Ik haastte mij, u haastte u	ik **hahs**te may, ew **hahs**te ew
I will hurry	Ik zal mij haasten	ik zahl may **hahs**ten
I am not in a hurry	Ik heb geen haast	ik hep khayn hahst
I ask for help	Ik vraag hulp	ik vrahkh hewlp
You ask for help	U vraagt hulp	ew vrakht hewlp
I asked for help	Ik vroeg hulp	ik vrookh hewlp
You asked for help	u vroeg hulp	ew vrookh hewlp
I am not asking for help	Ik vraag geen hulp	ik vrahkh khayn hewlp
Passport	Paspoort	**pass**port
Flight	Vlucht	vlewkht
Outgoing flight	Vertrekkende vlucht	ver**trekk**ende vlewkht
Following flight	Volgende vlucht	**vol**khende vlewkht
Flight number	Vlucht nummer	**vlewkht**-newmer
Suitcase, customs	Koffer, douane	**kof**fer, doo**ahn**
Money	Geld	khelt

9

FIRST MEETING; GREETINGS

English	EERSTE KENNISMAKEN; GROETEN	AYRSTE KENNISMAHKEN; KHROOTEN
Good morning	Goede morgen	khoode morkhen
Good evening	Goede avond	khoode ahvont
Good night	Goede nacht	khoode nahkht
Welcome!	Welkom	velkom
My name is ...	Mijn naam is	mayn nahm is
I am from the United-States	Ik kom uit Amerika	ik kom aewt amerika
I speak only English	Ik spreek alleen Engels	ik sprayk ahlayn engels
I am pleased to meet you	Aangenaam kennismaken	ahnkhenahm kenismahken
How are you?	Hoe maakt u het?	hoo mahkt ew het?
Thank you, And how are you?	Dank u, en u?	dahnk ew, en ew?
How are things?	Hoe gaat het er mee?	hoo khaht het er may?
All right	Goed	khoot
I've come to learn about your country	Ik kwam om iets over u land te leren	ik kvam om eets over ew lant te layren

10

English	Dutch	Pronunciation
I've come on a vacation	Ik kwam op vacantie	ik kwam op va**kant**see
Is there someone here who speaks English?	Spreekt er hier iemand Engels?	spraykt er heer **ee**mahnt **eng**els?
Yes; No	Ja, nee	yah, nay
I don't speak Dutch	Ik spreek geen Nederlands	ik sprayk khayn **nay**derlants
I speak English	Ik spreek Engels	ik sprayk **eng**els
I speak a little	Ik spreek een beetje	ik sprayk ayn **bayt**-ye
Do you understand me?	Begrijpt u mij?	be**khrayp**t ew may
I understand a little	Ik begrijp een beetje	ik be**khrayp** ayn **bayt**-ye
Pardon, excuse me	Pardon	par**doh**
I am sorry	Het spijt mij	het spayt may
It doesn't matter	Doet er niet toe	doot er neet too
Thank you very much	Dank u wel	dahnk ew vel
Don't mention it	Niets te danken	neets te **dahnk**en
What do you want?	Wat wilt u?	vat vilt ew?
I would like to visit the city	Ik wil de stad bezoeken	ik vil de stat be**zoo**ken
Wait a minute!	Een ogenblik	ayn **ohk**henblik
Come with me!	Kom met mij mee	kom met may may

I have to leave now	Ik moet nu gaan	ik moot new khahn
Thank you for your attention	Dank u voor uw aandacht	dahnk ew for ew **ahn**dakht
Good luck!	Succes	sewk**ses**
See you later!	Tot ziens	toht seens
Goodbye!	Dag	dahkh

HOTEL

HOTEL

HOTEL

I am looking for a good hotel	Ik zoek een goed hotel	ik zook ayn khoot ho**tel**
I am looking for an inexpensive hotel	Ik zoek een goedkoop hotel	ik zook ayn khoot**kohp** hotel
I booked a room here. Is it ready?	Ik heb een kamer bij u besproken. Is hij klaar?	ik hep ayn **kah**mer bay ew be**sproken**. is hay klahr?
Have you a single room?	Heeft u een één-persoonskamer?	hayft ew ayn **ayn**-per**sohns-kah**mer?
A double room?	Een tweepersoonskamer?	ayn tvay-per**sohns-kah**mer?
Have you a better room?	Heeft u een betere kamer?	hayft ew ayn **bay**tere **kah**mer?
Is the room air-conditioned?	Is de kamer airconditioned?	is de **kah**mer 'airconditioned'?

12

Does the room have a shower?	Heeft de kamer een douche?	hayft de **kah**mer ayn doosh?
With breakfast?	Met ontbijt?	met ont-**bayt?**
How much is the room?	Wat kost de kamer?	vat kost de **kah**mer?
I should like to see the room	Kan ik de kamer zien?	kan ik de **kah**mer zeen?
Do you have something bigger? Smaller? Cheaper? Quieter?	Heeft u iets groters? kleiners? Goedkopers? Rustigers?	hayft ew eets **khroh**ters? **klay**ners? khoot-**ko**pers? **rews**tikhers?
Will you send for my bags?	Wilt u mijn bagage sturen?	vilt ew mayn ba**khah**zhe **stew**ren?
I would like to keep this in the safe	Ik wou dit graag in de safe bewaren	ik vow dit khrahkh in de 'safe' be**vah**ren
Where is the ladies' room? The men's room?	Waar is het dames toilet? Waar is het heren toilet?	vahr is het **dah**mes twah**let?** vahr is het **hay**ren twah**let?**
Where is the dining room? T.V. Room?	Waar is de eetzaal? T.V.-zaal?	vahr is de **ayt**zahl? ... tele**vee**zee zahl
Please, wake me at ...	Wilt u mij om ... wekken?	vilt ew may om ... **vek**ken?

13

Who's there? Please wait! Come in!	Wie is daar? Wacht alstublieft! Binnen!	vee is dahr? vakht alstewbleeft! binnen!
May I have another towel?	Heeft u nog een handdoek voor mij?	hayft ew nokh ayn hant-dook for may?
May I have another pillow?	Heeft u een ander kussen voor mij?	hayft ew ayn ander kewssen for may?
...another blanket?	...een andere deken?	...ayn andere dayken?
...hangers?	...klerenhangers?	...klayren-hangers?
...hot water bottle?	...kruik?	...kraewk?
...night lamp?	...nachtlampje?	...nakht-lampye?
...needle and thread?	...naald en draad?	...nahlt en draht?
...writing paper? pen?	...schrijfpapier en pen?	...srayf-papeer en pen?
Could you cable abroad for me?	Kunt u een telegram voor mij sturen naar het buitenland?	kewnt ew ayn telekhram for may nahr het baewtenlant stewren?
A vacant room	Een vrije kamer	ayn fraye kahmer
Receptionist	Receptionist	resepsyonist
Chambermaid	Kamermeisje	kahmer-mayshe

14

Security Officer	Veiligheids officier	**vay**likh-hayts ofi**seer**
Waiter	Kellner	**kel**ner
Dining Room	Eetzaal	**ayt**zahl
Reception room	Lounge	'lounge'
Lift boy (Elevator boy)	Liftbediende	**lift**-bedeende
Room key	Kamersleutel	**kah**merslaytel
Room number	Kamernummer	**kah**mer-newmer
Bed	Bed	bet
Blanket	Deken	**day**ken
Sheet	Laken	**lah**ken
Men's toilet.	Heren W.C.	**hay**ren vay-say
Ladies' toilet	Dames W.C.	**dah**mes vay-say
Toilet paper	W.C.papier	vay-say pa**peer**

INFORMATION AT HOTEL

INLICHTINGEN IN HET HOTEL

Is there a taxi station nearby?

Waar is een taxi standplaats in de buurt?

vahr is ayn taxi **stant**plahts in de bewrt?

English	Dutch	Pronunciation
What is the telephone number?	Wat is het telefoonnummer?	vat is het tele**fohn**-newmer?
How do I get to ...?	Hoe kom ik naar...?	hoo kom ik nahr...?
By bus?	Met de bus?	met de bewss?
Where is the bus stop?	Waar is de bushalte?	vahr is de **bews**-halte?
Where is the nearest post office?	Waar is een postkantoor in de buurt?	vahr is ayn postkan**tor** in de bewrt?
Ladies' hairdresser	Dameskapper	**dah**mes-kapper
Barber	Herenkapper	**hay**ren-kapper
Laundry, shop	Wasserij, winkel	vasse**ray**, **vink**el
Where can I get a snack?	Waar kan ik een hapje eten?	vahr kan ik ayn **hap**ye **ay**ten?
Is there a grocery nearby?	Waar is een kruidenier in deze buurt?	vahr is ayn kraewde**neer** in **day**ze bewrt?
Where is the Tourist Information Office?	Waar is de V.V.V.?	vahr is de vay-vay-vay?
Can I have a programme of this week's events?	Heeft u het weekprogramma voor mij?	hayft ew het **vayk**-prokhrahma for may?
How can I get to...?	Hoe kom ik bij...?	hoo kom ik bay...?

... on foot?	... lopend?	... **loh**pent?
...by bus?	...met de bus?	...met de bewss?
... to this address?	...naar dit adres?	...nahr dit **adress**?
... to the center of town?	...naar het centrum?	...nahr her **sen**trewm?
... to the shopping district?	...naar het winkelcentrum?	...nahr het **vink**elsentrewm?
... to a bookshop?	...naar een boekhandel?	...nahr ayn **book**handel?
... to the market?	...naar de markt?	...nahr de markt?
... to the exhibitions?	...naar de tentoonstelling?	...nahr de ten**tohn**-stelling?
... to the museum?	...naar het museum?	...nahr het mew**zay**um?
...to the theatre?	...naar de schouwburg?	...nahr de **skhow**-burkh?
... to the cinema?	...naar de bioscoop?	...nahr de bee-o-**skohp**?
... to a nightclub?	...naar een nachtclub?	...nahr ayn **nakht**-klewp?
What plays are running this week?	Wat is er deze week in de schouwburg?	vat is er **day**ze vayk in de **skhow**-burkh?
Which films worth seeing are on this week?	Wat zijn er deze week voor films die de moeite waard zijn?	vat zayn er **day**ze vayk for films dee de **mooy**-te vahrt zayn?

17

English	Dutch	Pronunciation
Is there a tennis court nearby?	Is er een tennisbaan in de buurt?	is er ayn **ten**nisbahn in de bewrt?
Have you got any mail for me?	Zijn er brieven voor mij gekomen?	zayn er **bree**ven vor may khe**kom**en?
Is there a message for me?	Is er een bericht voor mij gekomen?	is er ayn be**rikht** vor may khe**kom**en?
I am going out and will return at …	Ik ga weg en kom om … uur terug	ik khah vekh en kom om …ewr trewkh
I'll leave the hotel tomorrow at …	Morgen om … uur verlaat ik het hotel	**mor**khen om …ewr ver**laht** ik het ho**tel**
Please make up my bill	Wilt u de rekening klaarmaken?	vilt ew de **ray**kening **klahr**mahken?
May I store my luggage here until … ?	Kan ik mijn bagage hier laten tot …?	kan ik mayn ba**khah**zhe heer **lah**ten tot…
Goodbye	Tot ziens	tot seens

TAXI

English	Dutch	Pronunciation
Please call me a taxi.	Wilt u een taxi voor mij bestellen?	vilt ew ayn taxi for may be**stellen?**
Driver would you please bring my suitcase inside?	Chauffeur, wilt u mij met mijn koffer helpen?	'chauffeur', vilt ew may met mayn **koffer hel**pen?
Take me to this address, please ...	Wilt u mij naar dit adres brengen?	vilt ew may nahr dit a**dress brengen?**
Please drive more slowly	Wilt u iets langzamer rijden?	vilt ew eets **lang**zahmer **ray**den?
How much is the fare?	Wat is het tarief?	vat is het ta**reef?**
Can you come here at ... in order to take me back?	Kunt u om ... hier komen om me terug te brengen?	kewnt ew om ...heer **ko**men om me trewkh te **breng**en?

IN THE POST OFFICE / IN HET POSTKANTOOR / IN HET POST-KAN**TOHR**

English	Dutch	Pronunciation
Where is the post office?	Waar is het postkantoor?	vahr is het postkan**tohr?**
Where can I send an overseas cable?	Bij welk loket kan ik een telegram naar het buitenland sturen?	bay velk lo**ket** kan ik ayn tele**khrahm** nahr het **baew**tenlant **stew**ren?

19

Please, give me an overseas cable form	Ik wil graag een formulier hebben om naar het buitenland te sturen	ik vil khrahkh ayn formew-**leer heb**ben om nahr het **baew**tenlant te **stewr**en
Have I written the telegram clearly?	Heb ik het telegram duidelijk geschreven?	hep ik het tele**khrahm daew**delek khes**khray**ven?
How much do I have to pay?	Wat moet ik betalen?	vat moot ik bet**ah**len?
What stamps do I need for this letter?	Wat moet ik aan postzegels opplakken voor deze brief?	vat moot ik ahn **post**-zaykhels **op**lakken for **day**ze breef?
...by surface mail?	...per zeepost?	...per **zay**post?
...by air mail?	...per luchtpost?	...per **lewkht**-post?
...by registered mail?	...als aangetekende brief?	**...als ahn**khetay**kende** breef?
...by express delivery?	...als expres brief?	...als expres breef?
Please send this by registered mail	Wilt u dit aangetekend sturen?	vilt ew dit **ahn**khetay**kend stewr**en?
Please give me... postcards	Geeft u mij ... ansichtkaarten	khayft ew may ... **an**sikht-karten
Give me airletters to Europe, to America, please	Ik wil graag een luchtbrief voor Europa, Amerika hebben	ik vil khrahkh ayn **lewkht**-breef for ew**roh**pa, ame**ri**ka, **heb**ben

Where is the nearest post box ?	Waar is de dichtst bijzijnde brievenbus?	vahr is de **dikh**tst-bayzaynde **bree**venbews?
May I have some telephone tokens, please?	Ik wil graag telefoonmunten hebben	ik vil khrahkh tele**fohn**-mewnten **heb**ben
Please, could you get me this number, as I could not get it by dialing?	Wilt u mij met het volgende nummer verbinden?	vilt ew may met het **fol**khende **new**mer ver**bind**en?
	Want ik kreeg geen verbinding via de publieke telefoon	vant ik kraykh khayn ver-**bind**ing vee-a de pew**blee**ke tele**fohn**
Please, could you put me through to the International Exchange for this number?	Ik wil met dit nummer in het buitenland verbonden worden	ik vil met dit **new**mer in het **baew**tenland ver**bond**en **vor**den
Please book me a call for tomorrow at ...	Wilt u een gesprek voor mij aanvragen voor morgen om ... uur?	vilt ew ayn khe**sprayk** for may **ahn**vrahkhen for **mor**khen om ... ewr?
I've come for my overseas call, booked for ... (hr.)	Ik kom voor een gesprek naar het buitenland, dat vastgesteld is voor ... uur	ik kom for ayn khe**sprayk** nahr het **baew**tenland, dat **fast**-khestelt is for ... ewr

English	Dutch	Pronunciation
I'll be waiting here. Please call me when you get the connection	Ik wacht hier Roept u mij als u verbinding heeft	ik vakht heer roopt ew may als ew ver-**bin**ding hayft
How much do I have to pay?	Hoeveel moet ik betalen?	hoo**vayl** moot ik be**tah**len?
Please, may I have a receipt?	Kan ik een ontvangstbewijs krijgen?	kan ik ayn ont**vangs**-be**vayss kray**khen?
Thank you, goodbye	Dank u, tot ziens	dahnk ew, tot seens

IN THE RESTAURANT
IN HET RESTAURANT
IN HET RESTORAHN

English	Dutch	Pronunciation
I am hungry	Ik heb honger	ik hep **honger**
I am thirsty	Ik heb dorst	ik hep dorst
Where is there a good restaurant?	Waar is een goed restaurant?	vahr is ayn khoot resto**rahn**?
Waiter	Kellner	**kel**ner
Waitress	Juffrouw	**yer**frow
Can I see the menu?	Het menu, alstublieft	het me**new** alstew**bleeft**

English	Dutch	Pronunciation
Breakfast	Ontbijt	**ont**bayt
Lunch	Lunch	lewnsh
Dinner	Avondeten	**ah**vont-**ay**ten
I would like to order	Ik wil graag bestellen	ik vil khrahkh be**stellen**
Give me this	Wilt u dit mij geven?	vilt ew may dit **khay**ven?
Tea with lemon, tea with milk	Twee met citroen, melk	tay met see**troon, mel**ek
Coffee and milk	Koffie met melk	koffee met **mel**ek
Turkish coffee	Turkse koffie	**tewrske** ko**fee**
Nescafe and milk	Nescafe met melk	neska**fay** met **mel**ek
Milk, cocoa, espresso	Melk, cacao, espresso	melk, **kakow, espres**so
Cold, warm, hot	Koud, warm, heet	kowt, vahrm, hayt
Cold water, soda water	Koud water, soda water	kowt **vah**ter, soda **vah**ter
Orange juice, grapefruit juice	Sinaasappel, grapefruit sap	**see**nass-appel, 'grapefruit' sahp
Cake, ice-cream	Cafe, ijs	ka**fay**, ays
White beer, black beer	Wit bier, donker bier	vit beer, **donk**er beer
Sweet wine, dry wine	Zoete wijn, droge wijn	**zoo**te vayn, **drohk**he vayn
Cognac, whisky, arak	Cognac, whisky, arak	**kon**yak, **wiskee**, **a**rak

Buttered roll	Broodje met boter	**brohd**ye met **bo**ter
Roll and margarine	Broodje met margarine	**brohd**ye met markhareena
White bread, black bread	Wit brood, bruin brood	vit broht, braewn broht
Pita, toast and jam	Pita, toast met jam	**pee**ta, 'toast' met 'jam'
Rolls, pretzels	Broodjes, beigel	**brohd**yes, **beig**el
Egg, soft-boiled egg	Ei, zacht gekookt ei	ay, zakht khe**kohkt** ay
Omelette, fried egg	Ommelet, gebakken ei	ome**let**, khe**bak**ken ay
White cheese, yellow cheese	Witte kaas, gele kaas	**vit**te kahs, **khay**le kahs
Leben	Magere yoghurt	**mah**khere **yo**khert
Yogurt	Gewone yoghurt	khe**voh**ne **yo**khert
Sour cream	Bulgaarse yoghurt	bewl**khahr**se **yo**khert
Humous, tehina, beans	Houmous, tgina, bonen	**hoo**moos, te**hee**na, **boh**nen
Sausage, hot dogs	Worst, hot dog	vorst, 'hot dog'
Vegetable salad	Groentesla	**khroon**te-slah
Salt, oil, sugar	Zout, olie, suiker	zowt, **o**lee, **saew**ker
Pepper, lemon juice	Peper, citroensap	**pep**per, si**troon**-sahp
Olives, pickled cucumber	Olijven, gezouten komkommer	o**lay**ven, khe**zow**ten komkomer

Herring, pickled fish	Haring, gezouten vis	**hah**ring, khe**zow**ten vis
Smoked fish	Gerookte vis	khe**rohk**te vis
Filleted fish	Vis fillet	vis fi**lay**
Baked, filled carp	Gebakken, gevulde karper	khe**bakk**en, khe**vewl**de **kar**per
Baked, grilled, boiled	Gebakken, gegrilled, gekookt	khe**bakk**en, khe**grill,** khe**kohkt**
Fried, steamed	Gebakken, gestoomd	khe**bakk**en, khe**stohmt**
Chicken, turkey, duck	Kip, kalkoen, eend	kip, kal**koon**, aynt
Beef	Rundvlees	**rewnd**vlayss
Lamb	Lam	lahm
Liver, tongue	Lever, tong	**lay**ver, tong
Steak, shnitzel	Biefstuk, schnitzel	**beef**stewk, **shnits**el
Meat balls	Gehaktballen	khe**hakt**-ballen
Beans soup, vegetable soup	Bonensoep, groentesoep	**bohn**en-soop, **khroon**te-soop
Chicken soup, meat soup	Kippesoep, vleessoep	**kipp**e-soop, **vlays**-soop
Mashed potatoes	Puree	pew**ray**
Chips	Patates, frites	pa**taht** freet
Fruit salad	Fruitsla	**fraewt**-slah
Pudding	Pudding	**pu**dding

English	Dutch	Pronunciation
Glass, bottle, cup	Glas, fles, kop	khlass, fles, kop
Spoon, fork, knife	Lepel, vork, mes	**lay**pel, vork, mess
Plate, teaspoon	Bord, teelepel	bort, **tay**laypel
Serviette, ashtray	Servet, asbak	ser**vet,** asbak
Toothpicks	Tandenstokers	tah**nden-**stokers
How much must I pay?	Hoeveel moet ik betalen?	hoo**vayl** moot ik be**tah**len?
Change and a receipt, please	Wisselgeld en de kwitantie alstublieft	**vissel**-khelt en de kvi**tan**see alstew**bleeft**

GROCERY — KRUIDENIER — KRAEWDENEER

English	Dutch	Pronunciation
White bread, brown bread	Wit brood, bruin brood	vit broht, braewn broht
Milk, leben, yogurt	Melk, magere yoghurt, gewone yoghurt	**mel**ek, **mah**khere **yok**hert, khe**voh**ne **yok**hert
Sour cream	Bulgaarse yoghurt	bewl**khar**se **yok**hert
White cheese	Witte kaas	**vit**te kahss
Yellow cheese, salt cheese	Gele kaas, zoute kaas	khayle kahss, **zow**te kahss

26

English	Dutch	Pronunciation
Butter, margarine, oil	Boter, margarine, olie	**bo**ter, markha**reene**, **o**lee
Sardines	Sardientjes	sar**deen**tyes
Tuna fish, tuna salad	Tonijn, tonijnensla	to**nayn**, to**nayn**en-slah
Olives, eggs	Olijven, eieren	o**lay**ven, **ay**eren
Soup mix	Soep aroma	soop a**ro**ma
Sugar, honey, salt	Suiker, honing, zout	**saew**ker, **ho**ning, zowt
Preserved meat	Diepvries vlees	deep**vrees** vlayss
Laundry soap	Waspoeder	**vass**pooder
Flour, noodles	Meel, vermicelli	mayl, 'vermicelli'
Please give me	Geef mij alstublieft	khayf may alstew**bleeft**...
How much does...cost?	Hoeveel kost...?	hoo**vayl** kost ...?

27

FRUITS AND VEGETABLES	FRUIT EN GROENTE	FRAEWT EN **KHROONTE**
Almonds	Amandelen	**aman**delen
Apples	Appels	**ap**pels
Apricot	Abrikoos	abree**kohss**
Banana	Bananen	ba**nahn**
Beans	Bonen	**boh**nen
Beetroot	Beetwortel	**bayt**vortel
Cabbage	Kool	kohl
Carrot	Wortel	**vor**tel
Cauliflower	Bloemkool	**bloom**kohl
Corn	Graan	khrahn
Cucumber	Komkommer	kom**kom**mer
Dates	Dadels	**dah**dels
Eggplant	Aubergines	ohber**zheen**
Figs	Vijgen	**vay**gen
Garlic	Knoflook	**knof**lohk
Grapefruit	Grapefruit	'grapefruit'

Grapes	Druiven	**draew**ven
Lemon	Citroen	si**troon**
Lettuce	Sla	slah
Squash	Citroenkwast	si**troon**-kvahst
Melon	Meloen	me**loon**
Nuts	Noten	**noh**ten
Onion	Ui	aew
Oranges	Sinaasappelen	**seen**ass-appelen
Peaches	Perziken	per**zee**ken
Pears	Peren	**pey**ren
Peas	Erwten	**ehr**ten
Pepper	Peper	**pay**per
Pomegranate	Granaatappel	khra**naht**-appel
Potatoes	Aardappels	**ahrd**-appels
Radish	Radijs	ra**dayss**
Rice	Rijst	rayst
Spinach	Spinazie	spi**nah**zee
Tomatoes	Tomaten	to**mah**ten
Watermelon	Watermeloen	**vah**terme**loon**

BANK

English	Dutch	Pronunciation
Where is the nearest bank?	Waar is de dichtst bijzijnde bank?	vahr is de **dikh**st-bayzaynde bank?
I have dollars to exchange.	Ik moet dollars wisselen	ik moot **dol**lars **viss**elen
Travellers checks.	Reis checques	**rayss**-sheks
Will you please change... dollars into local currency for me?	Wilt u alstublieft ... dollars in plaatselijk geld voor mij wisselen?	vilt ew alstew**bleeft dol**lars in **plahts**elek khelt vor may **viss**elen?
Could I have it in small change, please? ... in large notes?	Ik wil graag kleingeld, grootgeld hebben	ik vil khrahkh **klayn**khelt, **khroht**-khelt **heb**ben
Could you, please, give me change for this note?	Wilt u dit biljet voor mij in kleingeld wisselen?	vilt ew dit bil**yet** vor may in **klayn**khelt **viss**elen?
Cash, checks	Contant, checques	kon**tant**, sheks
Clerk, manager	Ambtenaar, directeur	**am**tenahr, direk**tewr**
Cash desk, cashier	Kas, kassier	kahss, kas**seer**

CLOTHES	KLEREN	KLAYREN
I would like to buy...	Ik wilde graag... kopen	ik **vil**de khrahkh ...**koh**pen
My size is ...	Mijn maat is	mayn maht is...
May I try it on?	Mag ik het passen	makh ik het **pas**sen?
This is too short, too long	Dit is te kort, te lang	dit is te kort, te lahng
It is too tight, too loose	Het is te nauw, te wijd	het is te now, te vayt
I would like to have it shortened	Ik wou het korter gemaakt hebben	ik vow het **kor**ter khe**mahkt heb**ben
Shorts	Korte broek	**kor**te brook
Trousers	Lange broek	**lahng**e brook
Boots	Laarzen	**lahr**zen
Brassiere	Bustehouder	**bews**te-howder
Button	Knoop	knohp
Cape	Cape	'cape'
Coat	Jas	yahss
Collar	Kraag	khrahkh
Cotton material	Katoen	ka**toon**
Dress	Jurk	yewrk

31

Gloves	Handschoenen	**hant**-skhoone
Hat	Hoed	hoot
Handkerchief	Zakdoek	**zahk**-dook
Jacket	Jasje	**yah**she
Ladies' handbag	Damestas	**da**mestas
Leather	Leer	layr
Linen	Linnen	**li**nen
Nylon stockings	Nylon kousen	'nylon' **kow**sen
Night shirt	Nachthemd	**nakht**-hemt
Pocket	Zak	zahk
Pantyhose	Maillot	mah**yoh**
Pajamas	Pyama	pi**yah**ma
Raincoat	Regenjas	**ray**khen-yahss
Robe	Avondjurk	**ah**vont-yewrk
Rubber boots	Rubber laarzen	**rew**ber **lahr**zen
Sandals	Sandalen	san**dah**len
Scarf	Shawl	'shawl'
Scissors	Schaar	skhahr

English	Dutch	Pronunciation
Shoe laces	Veters	**vay**ters
Shoes	Schoenen	**skhoo**nen
Silk	Zij	zay
Skirt	Rok	rohk
Skullcap	Kap	kahp
Slippers	Instap schoenen	**in**stap skhoonen
Sports shoes, sneakers	Sport schoenen	sport **skhoo**nen
Stockings	Kousen	**kow**sen
Sweater	Trui	traew
Swimsuit	Zwempak	**zvem**pahk
Suit	Pak	pahk
Synthetic material	Kunststof	**kewnst**-stof
Belt	Riem	reem
Tie	Das	dahss
Umbrella	Parapluie	para**plew**
Underpants	Onderbroek	**on**derbrook
Velvet	Fluweel	flew-**vayl**
Undershirt, vest	Hemd	**hemt**
Woolen material	Wollen stof	**vol**len stof
Zipper	Ritssluiting	**rits**-slaewting

33

COLORS

I want a light shade
    Dark shade
Red, yellow
Green, blue
Purple, gray
Black, white
Brown, pink

KLEUREN

Ik wilde een lichte tint,
  donkere tint
Rood, geel
Groen, blauw
Paars, grijs
Zwart, wit
Bruin, roze

KLERREN

ik **vil**de ayn **likh**tere tint,
  donkere tint
roht, khayl
khroon, blow
pahrs, khrayss
zvahrt, vit
braewn, **roh**ze

LAUNDRY

Could you please clean my
    suit, coat, sweater?
Please, could you wash and
    iron the shirts and
    underwear for me?
When will they be ready for
    me?

WASSERIJ

Wilt u mijn pak, jas, trui
  stomen?
Wilt u deze overhemden en dit
  ondergoed voor mij wassen
  en strijken?
Wanneer kan ik het
  terugkrijgen?

VAHSSERAY

vilt ew mayn pahk, yahss,
  traew **stoh**men?
vilt ew **day**ze **o**verhemden en
  dit **o**nder-khoot vor may
  vassen en **stray**ken?
va**nayr** kan ik het te**rewkh**-
  kraykhen?

34

English	Dutch	Pronunciation
Please also do any necessary repairs	Wilt u maken wat gemaakt moet worden?	vilt ew **mahk**en vat khe**mahkt** moot **vor**den?
The belt of the dress is missing	De ceintuur van de jurk ontbreekt	de san**tewr** van de yewrk ont**braykt**

BOOKSHOP / BOEKHANDEL / BOOK-HANDEL

English	Dutch	Pronunciation
I would like to buy ...	Ik wil graag ...kopen	ik vil khrahkh ... **koh**pen
... a newspaper	...een krant	...ayn krant
... a magazine	...een tijdschrift	...ayn **tayts**-srift
... a guidebook	...een gids	...ayn khits
... a map of the city	...een kaart van de stad	...ayn kahrt van de stat
... a map of the country	...een kaart van het land	...ayn kahrt van het lant
... envelopes	...enveloppen	...enve**lop**pen
... a writing pad	...een bloknoot	...ayn **blok**noht
... an exercise book	...een werkboek	...ayn **verk**book
... a pencil	...een potlood	...ayn **pot**loht
... a fountain pen	...een vulpen	...ayn **vewl**pen
... a ballpoint pen	...een ballpoint	...ayn 'ballpoint'
... a refill for the pen	...een vulling	...ayn **vewl**ing

AT THE HAIR DRESSER	BIJ DE KAPPER	BAY DE KAHPER
I want to get a hair cut	Ik wil mijn haar laten knippen	ik vil mayn hahr **lah**ten **knip**pen
In front, on the sides, behind	Vooraan, aan de zijkant, achteraan	**vor**ahn, ahn de **zay**kant, **akh**terahn
Shorter, longer	Korter, langer	**kor**ter, **lahn**ger
Side locks, beard, moustache	Bakkebaarden, baard, snor	**bak**kebahrden, bahrt, snohr
How long must I wait?	Hoe lang moet ik wachten?	hoo lahng moot ik **vakh**ten?
A short while, a long time	Een ogenblik, lang	ayn **ohk**henblik, lahng
I want a shampoo, please	Shampoo alstublieft	**sham**poh alstew**bleeft**
The water is too hot	Het water is te heet	het **vah**ter is te hayt
I want a shave	Ik wil geschoren worden	ik vil khe**skho**ren **vor**den
Be careful here!	Hier voorzichtig alstublieft	heer vor**zikh**tikh alstew**bleeft**
I want my hair dyed	Ik wil mijn haar laten verven	ik vil mayn hahr **lah**ten **ver**ven
I want my hair set	Ik wil mijn haar laten wassen en watergolven	ik vil mayn hahr **lah**ten **vahs**en en **vah**ter-kholven
Pedicure, manicure	Pedicuur, manicuur	pedi**kewr**, mani**kewr**

THE WEATHER	HET WEER	HET VAYR
What a beautiful day!	Wat een prachtige dag!	vat ayn **prakh**tikhe dahkh!
Bright, the sun is shining	Helder, de zon schijnt	**hel**der, de zon skhaynt
Warm, hot, very hot	Warm, heet, erg heet	vahrm, hayt, erkh hayt
Chilly, cold, very cold	Kil, koud, erg koud	kil, kowt, erkh kowt
Dry, heat wave	Droog, hittegolf	drohkh, **hit**te kholf
Damp, drizzle, rain	Vochtig, motregen, regen	**vokh**tikh, **mot**raykhen, **ray**khen
Cloudy, foggy	Mistig	**mist**ikh
To wear a warm coat	Een warme jas dragen	ayn **vahr**me yahss **drah**khen

TRANSPORT	VERVOER	VERVOOR
Bus, train, plane	Bus, trein, vliegtuig	bews, trayn, **vleekh**-taewkh
Underground, fast train	Ondergrondse, sneltrein	**on**der-khrontse, **snel**trayn
Ticket, ticket office	Kaartje, loket	**kahr**tye, **lo**ket
Driver, steward, stewardess	Chauffeur, steward, stewardess	'chauffeur', 'steward', 'stewardess'

37

Load/luggage, porter	Vracht / bagage, kruier	vrakht / bakhazhe, **kraew**yer
Where is the lost baggage office?	Waar is het bureau voor gevonden voorwerpen?	vahr is het bew**roh** vor khe**vonde**n **vor**verpen
I left ... in the coach	Ik heb... verloren in de coupé	ik hep... ver**loren** in de koo**pay**

TRAIN, BUS

TREIN, BUS

TRAYN, BEWS

From where does the train for ... leave?	Hoe laat vertrekt de trein naar?	hoo laht ver**trekt** de trayn nahr...?
How do I get there?	Hoe kom ik daar?	hoo kom ik dahr?
By train, bus, underground (subway)	Met de trein, bus, ondergrondse	met de trayn, bewss, **on**der-khrontse?
Where is the ticket office?	Waar kan ik kaartjes kopen?	vahr kan ik **kahrt**yes **koh**pen?
At what time does the next train leave for ...?	Hoe laat vertrekt de volgende trein naar...?	hoo laht ver**trekt** de **vol**khende trayn nahr...?
Give me a ticket for ... please	Een kaartje naar... alstublieft	ayn **kahrt**ye nahr... alstew**bleeft**
If possible, by the window and facing the front	Een raamplaats, vooruit alstublieft	ayn **rahm**plahts, **vor**aewt alstew**bleeft**

English	Dutch	Pronunciation
Where can I find a porter?	Waar kan ik een kruier vinden?	vahr kan ik ayn **kraew**yer **vin**den?
Please, take the bags to the coach	Wilt u de bagage meenemen naar de coupé?	vilt ew de ba**kha**zhe **may**naymen nahr de koo**pay?**
Where is the dining coach?	Waar is de restauratiewagen?	vahr is de resto**raht**see-**vah**khen?
May I open (close) the window?	Mag ik het raam open (dicht) doen?	makh ik her rahm **o**pen (dikht) doon?
May I smoke?	Mag ik roken?	makh ik **roh**ken?
When does the train arrive at?	Hoe laat komt de trein aan?	hoo laht komt de trayn ahn?
What bus goes to...?	Welke bus gaat naar?	**vel**ke bews khaht nahr...?
Where is the bus to ...?	Waar is de bus naar?	vahr is de bews nahr ...?
How much is a ticket to ...?	Wat kost een kaartje naar...?	vat kost ayn **kahrt**ye nahr ...?
Is this the bus to ...?	Is dit de bus naar...?	is dit de bews nahr ...?
I am looking for this address	Ik zoek dit adres	ik zook dit **adress**
At which station do I get off?	Waar moet ik er uit?	vahr moot ik er aewt?

AIRPLANE	VLIEGTUIG	**VLEEKH**-TAEWKH
By which means of transport do I get to the airport?	Hoe kom ik naar het vliegveld?	hoo kom ik nahr het **vleekh**-velt?
Is there a bus service (taxi) to there?	Is er een bus (taxi) heen?	is er ayn bews (taxi) hayn?
At what time will I be picked up?	Hoe laat word ik afgehaald?	hoo laht vort ik **af**khehahlt?
Which is the nearest bus stop to the airport?	Waar is de dichtst bijzijnde halte voor het vliegveld?	vahr is de **dikhtst bay**zaynde **hal**te vor het **vleekh**-velt?
At what time should I be there?	Hoe laat moet ik er zijn?	hoo laht moot ik er zayn?
At what time does the plane take off?	Hoe laat vertrekt het vliegtuig?	hoo laht ver**trekt** het **vleekh**-taewkh?
When will it arrive?	Hoe laat komt het aan?	hoo laht komt het ahn?
Is there a flight to?	Is er een vlucht naar...?	is er ayn vlewkht nahr...?
What is the flight number?	Wat is het vlucht nummer?	vat is het vlewkht **new**mer?
I have nothing to declare	Ik heb niets aan te geven	ik hep neets ahn te **khay**ven
This is all I have	Dit is alles wat ik heb	dit is **all**es vat ik hep

English	Dutch	Pronunciation
Please, take my luggage	Wilt u mijn bagage nemen?	vilt ew mayn ba**kha**zhe **nay**men?
May I have a travel sickness pill, please?	Heeft u een pil tegen reisziekte voor mij?	hayft ew ayn pil **tay**khen **rays**seekte vor may?
May I have a glass of water?	Heeft u een glas water voor mij?	hayft ew ayn khlahs **vah**ter vor may?

CAR JOURNEY / AUTOREIS / OHTOH-RAYSS

English	Dutch	Pronunciation
Where can I rent a car?	Waar kan ik een auto huren?	vahr kan ik ayn **oh**toh **hew**ren?
I have an international driving license	Ik heb een internationaal rijbewijs	ik hep ayn internasho**nahl ray**be-vayss
How much is it to rent a car per day?	Wat kost een dag auto huren?	vat kost ayn dahkh **oh**toh **hew**ren?
What is the additional rate per kilometer?	Wat moet ik per kilometer bijbetalen?	vat moot ik per **ki**lomayter **bay**-betahlen?
Where is the nearest petrol (gas) station?	Waar is het dichtst bijzijnde benzinestation?	vahr is het **dikhst**-bayzaynde ben**zeene**-stahshohn?

41

Please, put in ... liters	...liter benzine alstublieft	... 'liter' benzeene alstewbleeft
Check the oil, please	Wilt u de motorolie controleren?	vilt ew de motor-olee kontrolayren?
... the brakes	...Remolie	...remohlee...
... the gear box	Olie van de versnellingsbak	olee van de versnellingsbahk
Please put water in the battery, radiator	Wilt u water in de accu, radiator doen?	vilt ew vahter in de akew, radiahtor doon?
Change the oil in the car, please	Wilt u de auto doorsmeren?	vilt ew de ohtoh dohrsmayren?
May I have a road map of the area?	Heeft u een autokaart van de omgeving?	hayft ew ayn ohtoh-kahrt van de omkhayving?
Please inflate the tires, the reserve wheel too	Wilt u de banden en de reserveband oppompen?	vilt ew de banden en de rezervebant op-pompen?
Please repair the puncture	Wilt u de lekke band repareren?	vilt ew de lekke bant reparayren?
Please change the inner tube, the tire	Wilt u de binnenband verwisselen?	vilt ew de binnenbant vervisselen?
What is the speed limit?	Wat is de snelheidsgrens?	vat is de snelhayts-khrents?

English	Dutch	Pronunciation
Which is the way to …?	Wat is de weg naar…?	vat is de vekh nahr…?
Is that a good road?	Is dat een goede weg?	is dat ayn **khoo**de vekh?
Is there a shorter way?	Is er een kortere weg?	is er ayn **kor**tere vekh?
Which place is this?	Welke plaats is dit?	**vel**ke plahts is dit?
Is this the road to …?	Is dit de weg naar…?	is dit de vekh nahr…?
Yes, no	Ja, nee	yah, nay
Please, go back	Gaat u terug	khaht ew **trewkh**
Go straight on	Recht door	rekht dohr
Turn to the right (left)	Rechtsaf, linksaf	**rekhts** af, **links** af
Turn to the north, (south, east, west)	Gaat u naar het noorden (zuiden, oosten, westen)	khaht ew nahr het **nor**den (**zaewd**en, **ohs**ten, **vest**en)
This way	Deze kant op	**day**ze kant op
That way	Die kant op	dee kant op
How far is it to …?	Hoever is het naar…?	hoo**ver** is het nahr…?
Is it near? (far?)	Is het dichtbij? (ver weg?)	is het dikht**bay**? ver vekh?
Very far?	Erg ver weg?	erkh ver vekh?
There, here	Daar, hier	dahr, heer

English	Dutch	Pronunciation
Please show me on the map	Wilt u het mij op de kaart laten zien?	vilt ew het may op de kahrt **lah**ten zeen?
Where are we?	Waar zijn wij?	vahr zayn vay?
Where is the place that we want to go to?	Waar is de plaats waar we naar toe willen gaan?	vahr is de plahts vahr vay nahr too **vill**en khahn?
On which road should we travel?	Welke weg moeten we nemen?	**velke** vekh **mooten** vay **nay**men?

TRAFFIC SIGNS   VERKEERSTEKENS   VERKAYRSTAYKENS

English	Dutch	Pronunciation
Stop!	Stop	stop!
Caution!	Oppassen	**op**-passen!
Dangerous curve	Gevaarlijke bocht	khe**vahr**leke bokht
Slow!	Langzaam	**lahng**zahm!
Danger!	Gevaar	khe**vahr**
First Aid	Eerste hulp	**ayr**ste hewlp
Red Cross	Rode kruis	**roh**de kraewss
Pharmacy	Apoteek	apo**tayk**
Police	Politie	po**leet**see

English	Dutch	Pronunciation
Bomb disposal pit	Bomvrije kuil	**bom**vraye kaewl
Fire hydrant	Brandspuit	**brant**spaewt
No parking	Verboden te parkeren	ver**boh**den te par**kayr**en
No entry	Verboden in te rijden	ver**boh**den in te **ray**den
No crossing	Verboden over te steken	ver**boh**den over te **stay**ken
One-way Street	Eenrichtingsverkeer	**ayn**rikhtings-ver**kayr**
Pedestrian crossing	Voetgangers oversteek plaats	**voot**khangers-**o**verstayk-plahts
Detour	Omleiding	**om**layding
Travel on this road	Rijd op deze weg	rayt op **dayze** vekh
Go slow	Rijd langzaam	rayt **lang**zahm
Take care	Pas op	pas op!
Crossroad, junction	Zijweg, kruispunt	**zay**vekh, **kraews**pewnt
Bridge, highway	Brug, hoofdweg	brewkh, **hohft**-vekh
Dual highway	Tweebaans hoofdweg	**tvay**bahns **hohft**-vekh
Bad road	Slechte weg	**slekh**te vekh
Narrow road	Smalle weg	**smah**le vekh
Road under repair	Opgebroken weg	**op**khebroken vekh
Dirt road	Onverharde weg	**on**verhahrde vekh

45

Steep incline	Steile helling	**stayle** **hel**ling
Steep decline	Steile afdaling	**stayle** **af**dahling
Sharp turn	Scherpe bocht	**skher**pe bokht
Blinding light	Verblindend	ver**blind**end likht
Children on the road	Kinderen op straat	**kind**eren op straht
Men at Work	Mensen aan het werk	**men**sen ahn het verk
Right	Rechts	rekhts
Left	Links	links
Entrance	Ingang	**ink**hang
Exit	Uitgang	**aewt**khang
No smoking	Verboden te roken	ver**boh**den te **roh**ken
Information	Inlichtingen	**in**likhtingen
Elevator	Lift	lift
Restrooms	Wachtkamers	**vakht**-kahmers
Men	Heren	**hay**ren
Women	Dames	**dah**mes
For sale	Te koop	te kohp
For rent	Te huur	te hewr

46

GARAGE	GARAGE	KHARAZHE
Where is a garage nearby?	Waar is een garage in de buurt?	vahr is ayn kharazhe in de bewrt?
Please check and adjust the brakes	Wilt u de remmen controleren en bijstellen?	vilt ew de **rem**men kontro**leer**en en **bay**stellen?
Please check the gearbox and adjust the clutch	Wilt u de versnelling en de koppeling nakijken?	vilt ew de ver**snel**ling en de **kop**peling **nah**kayken?
The engine uses too much oil	De motor verbruikt te veel olie	de **mo**tor ver**braewkt** te vayl **o**lee
The engine is overheating	De motor wordt gauw heet	de **mo**tor vort khow hayt
The radiator needs refilling too often	Er ontbreekt te vaak water in de radiator	er ont**braykt** te vahk **vah**ter in de radi**ah**tor
Please check the plugs	Wilt u de bougies controleren?	vilt ew de boo**zhee** kontro**leer**en?
Please check the points	Wilt u de contactpunten controleren?	vilt ew de kon**takt**-pewnten contro**leer**en?
The car doesn't start well	De auto start niet goed	de **oh**toh start neet khoot
Please check the headlight alignment	Wilt u de koplampen controleren?	vilt ew de **kop**lampen kontro**leer**en?

47

REPAIRS	REPARATIES	REPARAHTSEES
Wheel balance	Wielen uitbalanceren	**veele**n aewt-balan**sayre**n
Oil change	Doorsmeren	dohr-**smayre**n
Tighten screws	Schroeven aandraaien	sr**oove**n **ahn**drahyen
Fill the radiator	Vul de radiator	vewl de radi**ah**tor
Oil the engine	Smeer de motor	smayr de **mo**tor
Wheel alignment	Wielrichting	**veel**rikhting
Water for the battery	Water voor de accu	**vah**ter vor de **ake**w
The gear is stuck	De versnelling zit vast	de ver**snel**ling zit vast
...grinding	...kraakt	...krahkt
The oil is leaking	De olie lekt	de **ole**e lekt
The part is burnt out	Dit deel is verbrand	dit dayl is ver**brant**
To take a wheel apart	Een wiel eraf halen	ayn veel er**ahf hah**len
Short circuit	Kortsluiting	**kort**-slaewting
The steering wheel is loose	Het stuur zit los	het stewr zit loss
The axle rod is broken	De as is gebroken	de ahss is khe**broke**n
Puncture in the tire	Lekke band	**lek**ke bant
Everything is O.K.	Alles is in orde	**all**es is in **or**de

PARTS OF A CAR	AUTO-ONDERDELEN	OHTOH-ONDERDAYLEN
Battery	Accu	akew
Brakes	Remmen	remmen
Carburetor	Carburator	karbewrahtor
Clutch	Koppeling	koppeling
Distilled water	Gedestilleerd water	khedistileert vahter
Filter	Filter	filter
Gear	Versnelling	versnelling
Ignition	Ontsteking	ontstayking
Lubrication	Smeren	smayren
Pedal	Pedaal	pedahl
Piston	Zuiger	zaewkher
Radiator	Radiator	radiahtor
Spark plugs	Contactpunten	kontakt-pewnten
Spring	Veer	vayr
Steering wheel	Stuur	stewr
Wheel, wheels	Wiel, wielen	veel, veelen

PHYSICIANS

Where does an English speaking doctor live?

I need first aid

I need an internal specialist

Can you recommend a good doctor?

DOKTOREN

Waar woont een dokter die engels spreekt?

Ik heb eerste hulp nodig

Ik heb een internist nodig

Kunt u een goede dokter aanbevelen?

DOKTOHREN

vahr vohnt ayn **dok**ter dee **eng**els spraykt?

ik hep **ayr**ste hewlp **noh**dikh

ik hep ayn inter**nist noh**dikh

kewnt ew ayn **khoo**de **dok**ter ahnbe**vay**len?

TYPES OF DOCTORS

Ear, nose and throat specialist

Orthopedist

Surgeon

Pediatrician

Gynecologist

Dermatologist

Eye specialist

Neurologist

SOORTEN DOKTOREN

Oor—, neus- en keelarts

Ortopeed

Chirurg

Kinderarts

Vrouwenarts

Huidarts

Oogarts

Zenuwarts

SOHRTEN DOKTOHREN

ohr-nerss-en-**kayl**-ahrts

orto**payt**

shee**rewrkh**

kinder-ahrts

vrowen-ahrts

haewt-ahrts

ohkh-ahrts

zaynew-ahrts

English	Dutch	Pronunciation
Internal specialist	Internist	inter**nist**
Dentist	Tandarts	**tant**-ahrts

ILLNESSES ZIEKTES **ZEEKTES**

English	Dutch	Pronunciation
I have no appetite	Ik heb geen trek	ik hep khayn trek
Nausea	Misselijkheid	**miss**elek-hayt
Infection	Infectie	in**fek**see
Depression	Depressie	de**pres**see
Cold	Verkoudheid	ver**kowt**-hayt
Vomiting	Overgeven	over-khayven
Pregnancy, pregnant	Zwangerschap, zwanger	**zvang**er-skhahp, **zvang**er
Contraction	Kramp	kramp
Heart patient	Hartpatient	**hart**-pashent
Fever	Koorts	kohrts
Ulcer	Maagzweer	**makh**-zvayr

PARTS OF THE BODY	LICHAAMSDELEN	LIKHAHMS-DAYLEN
Ankle	Enkel	**enke**l
Appendix	Blinde darm	**blin**de darm
Arm	Arm	arm
Artery	Slagader	**slakh**-ahder
Back	Rug	rewkh
Bladder	Blaas	blahss
Blood	Bloed	bloot
Bone, bones	Bot, botten	bot, **bot**ten
Breast	Borst	borst
Chest	Borst	borst
Ear	Oor	ohr
Elbow	Elleboog	**elle**bohkh
Eye, eyes	Oog, ogen	ohkh, **ohkh**en
Finger	Vinger	**vin**ger
Foot, feet	Voet, voeten	voot, **voo**ten
Gland	Klier	kleer
Hand	Hand	hant

52

English	Dutch	Pronunciation
Head	Hoofd	hohft
Heart	Hart	hart
Heel	Hak	hahk
Hip, hips	Heup, heupen	herrp, **herrp**en
Intestine, intestines	Darm, darmen	darm, **darm**en
Joints	Gewrichten	khe**vrikht**en
Kidney, kidneys	Nier, nieren	neer, **neer**en
Knee	Knie	knee
Leg	Been	bayn
Liver	Lever	**lay**ver
Lungs	Longen	**long**en
Mouth	Mond	mont
Muscle	Spier	speer
Neck	Nek	nek
Nerve, nerves	Zenuw, zenuwen	**zay**new, **zay**newen
Nose	Neus	newss
Palm	(Hand) palm	(hant) palm

Rib, ribs	Rib, ribben	rip, **ribben**
Shoulder	Schouder	**skhow**der
Skin	Huid	haewt
Spine	Ruggegraat	**rewkhe**khraht
Stomach	Buik	baewk
Throat	Keel	kayl
Thumb	Duim	daewm
Tongue	Tong	tong
Tooth, Teeth	Tand, tanden	tahnt, **tahnd**en
Tonsil	Keelamandel, tonsil	**kayl**amandel, tonsil
Urine	Urine	ewreene
Vein	Ader	**ahder**

PHARMACY	APOTEEK	APOTAYK
Where is the nearest pharmacy?	Waar is de dichtst bijzijnde apoteek?	vahr is de **dikhst**-bayzaynde apo**tayk?**
Which pharmacy is on duty tonight?	Welke apoteek heeft nachtdienst?	**velke** apo**tayk** hayft **nakht**deenst?
Have you a medicine for a headache?	Heeft u iets tegen hoofdpijn?	hayft ew eets **tay**khen **hohft**payn?
Toothache	Kiespijn	**kees**payn
Iodine, aspirin	Jodium, aspirien	**yoh**diewm, aspi**reen**
Valerian drops	Valeriaan	valeri**ahn**
Antiseptic cream	Antiseptische zalf	anti**sep**tise zahlf
Hot water bottle	Warme kruik	**vahr**eme kraewk
Heating pad	Beschermkap	be**skherm** kahp
Cottonwool	Watten	**vat**ten
Band-aid	Verband	ver**bant**
Thermometer	Termometer	**ter**momayter
I need first aid	Ik heb eerste hulp nodig	ik hep **ayr**ste hewlp **noh**dikh
What are his office hours?	Wat zijn zijn werktijden?	vat zayn zayn **verk**tayden?

TIME	TIJD	TAYT
What is the time?	Hoe laat is het?	hoo laht is het?
It is four o'clock	Het is vier uur	het is veer ewr
Five minutes past six	Vijf over zes	vayf over zes
Half past five	Half zes	hahlf zes
A quarter past seven, ten minutes to eight	Kwart over zeven, Tien voor acht	kvart over zayven, teen vor akht
Morning	Ochtend	okhtent
Midday	Middag	middakh
Evening, night	Avond, nacht	ahvont, nakht
Midnight	Middernacht	middernakht
Today, yesterday	Vandaag, gisteren	vandahkh, khisteren
The day before yesterday	Eergisteren	ayrkhisteren
Tomorrow	Morgen	morkhen
The day after tomorrow	Overmorgen	overmorkhen
A second, hour	Seconde, uur	sekonde, ewr
Quarter of an hour	Kwartier	kvarteer

Half an hour	Half uur	hahlf ewr
Forty minutes	Veertig minuten	vayrtikh minewten
Day, days	Dag, dagen	dahkh, dahkhen
Week, weeks	Week, weken	vayk, vayken
Month, months	Maand, maanden	mahnt, mahnden
Year, years	Jaar, jaren	yahr, yahren
Period of ... years	Periode van ...jaren	periohde van ... yahren
In a month	In een maand	in ayn mahnt
Early, I am early	Vroeg, ik ben vroeg	vrookh, ik ben vrookh
Late, I am late	Laat, ik ben laat	laht, ik ben laht

DAYS OF THE WEEK

	DAGEN VAN DE WEEK	DAHKHEN VAN DE VAYK
Sunday, Monday	Zondag, maandag	zondakh, mahndakh
Tuesday, Wednesday	Dinsdag, woensdag	dinzdakh, voonsdakh
Thursday, Friday	Donderdag, vrijdag	donderdakh, vraydakh
Saturday	Zaterdag	zahterdakh

MONTHS	**MAANDEN**	**MAHNDEN**
January, February	Januari, februari	yanewahree, febrewahree
March, April, May	Maart, april, mei	mahrt, ahpril, may
June, July, August	Juni, juli, augustus	yewnee, yewlee,
		owkhewstewss
September, October	September, oktober	september, oktober
November, December	November, december	november, daysember

SEASONS	**JAARGETIJDEN**	**YAHRKHETAYDEN**
Spring, Summer	Lente, zomer	lente, zomer
Autumn, Winter	Herfst, winter	herfst, vinter

NUMBERS	**GETALLEN**	**KHETAHLEN**
One, two	een, twee	ayn, tvay
Three, four	drie, vier	dree, veer
Five, six	vijf, zes	vayf, zes

Seven, eight	zeven, acht	**zay**ven, akht
Nine, ten	negen, tien	**nay**khen, teen
Eleven, twelve	elf, twaalf	elf, tvahlf
Thirteen, fourteen	dertien, veertien	**der**teen, **vayr**teen
Fifteen, sixteen	vijftien, zestien	**vayf**teen, **zes**teen
Seventeen, eighteen	zeventien, achtien	**zay**venteen, **akh**teen
Nineteen, twenty	negentien, twintig	**nay**khenteen, **tvin**tikh
Twenty-one, twenty-two	eenentwintig, tweeentwintig	**ay**nentvintikh, **tvay**entvintikh
Thirty, forty	dertig, veertig	**der**tikh, **vayr**tikh
Fifty, sixty, seventy	vijftig, zestig, zeventig	**vayf**tikh, **zes**tikh, **zay**ventikh
Eighty, ninety, one hundred	tachtig, negentig, honderd	**takh**tikh, **nay**khentikh, **hond**ert
One hundred and one	honderd een	hondert-ayn
Two hundred	twee honderd	**tvay** hondert
One thousand	duizend	**daew**zent
One thousand and one	duizend een	daewzent-ayn
Two thousand	tweeduizend	tvay-daewzent
Two thousand and one	tweeduizend een	tvay-daewzent-**ayn**
One million, billion	een miljoen, biljoen	ayn mil**yoon**, bil**yoon**

59

EMERGENCY EXPRESSIONS	NOODUITDRUKKINGEN	NOHT-AEWT-DREWKINGEN
Help!	Help!	help!
Stop, thief!	Houd de dief!	howt de deef!
Don't touch me!	Raak me niet aan!	rahk me neet ahn!
Leave me alone!	Laat me met rust!	laht me met rewst.
Call the police!	Roep de politie!	roop de po**leet**see!
I've lost my way.	Ik ben de weg kwijt geraakt	ik ben de vekh kvayt khe**rahkt.**
How do I get to this address ?	Hoe kom ik bij dit adres?	hoo kom ik bay dit **adress**?
Call me a taxi please	Wilt u een taxi laten komen?	vilt ew ayn taxi **lah**ten **ko**men?
I don't feel well.	Ik voel me niet goed.	ik vool me neet khoot.
Call a doctor!	Roep een dokter!	roop ayn **dok**ter.
Call an ambulance!	Roep een ziekenauto!	roop ayn **zeek**en-**oh**toh.
Take me to a first-aid station.	Breng me naar een E.H.B.O-post.	breng me nahr ayn ay-hah-bay-oh-post.
Take me to the hospital.	Breng me naar het ziekenhuis.	breng me nahr het **zeek**enhaews.
Take me to a doctor.	Breng me naar een dokter.	breng me nahr ayn **dok**ter.